Rose Garden

❧❧

A JOURNAL

by ANGELA KIRBY

Illustrated by ANNY EVASON

FRIEDMAN/FAIRFAX
PUBLISHERS

Contents

~v~

CHAPTER ONE

The History of the Rose

"Would you appoint some other flower to reign
In matchless beauty on the plain,
The Rose (mankind will all agree)
The Rose the Queen of Flowers should be."

Sappho, 650BC.

Roses come in many colors and shades. White roses are a symbol of purity and are often associated with the Virgin Mary. At dusk they can appear luminous, and are wonderfully fragrant in the evening air. A red rose is the flower of passion and romance. Legend tells that Aphrodite, running to the dying Adonis, was torn by a rose bush, and her blood, falling on the petals, painted them red for evermore. Others say that the blood of Adonis turned into red roses, or that they are the reflection of Venus, who blushed becomingly when Jupiter came upon her in her bath.

Roses are loved above all other flowers. They have been cultivated in many civilizations for thousands of years, prized for both their beauty and their perfume, and valued for their medicinal and culinary virtues. Celebrated in carvings, paintings, manuscripts, ballads, and poetry from the earliest recorded times, countless myths, legends, and superstitions have grown up around them—the ancients, for example, believed that anyone unfortunate enough to be transformed into an ass could be cured by feeding on rose petals.

*W*ild forms of the genus *Rosa* occur naturally only in the Northern hemisphere—in Asia, North Africa, North America, Europe, and the Middle East. Fossilized remains of roses found in these regions date back twenty- to thirty-million years. The cultivation of the rose is thought to have begun in the Middle East. Between 1920 and 1934, the archaeologist Sir Leonard Woolley carried out excavations at Ur, in southern Iraq, and found references to figs, vines, and roses, which had been brought back as booty almost 5000 years before, by King Sargon.

*R*ose-growing spread across Europe from the Middle East. Nobody is sure of the origins of the mysterious Holy Rose, or *Rosa sancta*, which was first found growing in Abyssinian religious courtyards. It belongs to the early group of summer damask roses, but seems to go back much farther in history than other garden roses. In 1888, archaeologist Sir Flinders Petrie found remains of rose garlands in early Egyptian tombs, and these proved to be *R. sancta*.

*S*ome of the earliest depictions of the rose were on jewelry and ornaments found in Crete, dating from the early Minoan civilization (2800-2100 BC), while roses were painted on the palace walls of ancient Crete in about 1600 BC. *The Iliad*, dating from around 1000 BC, contains what is supposedly the first literary reference to the rose, when Homer describes how Aphrodite anointed the fallen Hector with rose oil.

*R*oses were grown in Persia from early times, and were of great religious and cultural significance, often celebrated by the poets. *R. gallica* is believed to have been cultivated there in the 12th century BC. There were many famous gardens, including those at Shiraz, which was the home of two famous poets, Sa'adi in the 12th century AD, whose greatest work was *Gulistan* (*The Rose Garden*), and Hafiz, who, two centuries later, wrote of the rose: "*Grieve not; if the springtime of life should once more mount the throne of the garden, thou wilt soon see above thy head, O singer of the night, a curtain of roses.*" In the Chahar bagh, the 16th-century gardens of Isfahan, jasmine *(Jasminum officinale)*, poppies *(Papaver)*, and roses grew between rows of plane trees and poplars.

The Romans were not slow to follow the Greeks in the growing of roses, and soon surpassed them. They also devised many ways to use both roses and rose petals, weaving them into wreaths and garlands, strewing them over the floors of banqueting halls (the Emperor Heliogabulus is reputed to have strewn his guests with so many petals that some of them suffocated), making rose-scented anointing oils, scenting their baths, and making flavorings for both food and wine. Their passion for rose petals led to many Roman peasants turning over their cornfields to the more profitable growing of roses.

Legend has it that Cupid gave a rose to Harpocrates, the god of silence, bribing him to secrecy over the dalliances of Venus, and so the rose became the symbol of discretion. It was pictured on the ceilings of banqueting halls as a reminder that what was heard under them must not be repeated—hence the expression, *sub rosa* (under the rose), meaning, in strict secrecy.

The Roman writer, Pliny the Elder, in the 1st century AD, describes the growing of roses under glass in winter at Paestum, on the south-west coast of Italy, and notes that the necessary heat was provided by piped water. When the Romans wanted early roses, they imported large quantities of them from Africa, where they bloomed some two months earlier than in Italy.

The Chinese were lovers of the rose, and practiced its cultivation, possibly from 2000 BC. We know, too, from the works of the philosopher Confucius (551-479 BC), that roses were grown in the imperial gardens during the Chou dynasty. Only the ruling classes in China were allowed to use the prized rose oils. Today's hybrid roses owe their repeat-flowering habit to their Chinese ancestors.

Charlemagne, King of the Franks, and Emperor of Rome, was a fearless promoter of agriculture, commerce, and education. He issued a decree, the Capitulare de Villis, which included lists of plants to be grown on crown land—among them were fruits, herbs, nuts, roses, and vegetables.

The monasteries of the Middle Ages kept the art of gardening alive in Europe. A 10th-century plan of the St. Gall monastery in Switzerland shows a garden that is very similar to the Roman villa rustica, with orchards, herbs, and vegetables in separate rectangular beds, and other beds with flowers, including gladioli, lilies, and roses.

*I*n the early days of Christianity, the rose fell out of favor because of its connections with pagan rituals and Roman orgies, but it later became associated with the Virgin Mary (who is often referred to as "The Rose of Heaven" or "The Mystical Rose"), and many saints, including Angelus, Cassilda, Elizabeth of Portugal, Rosalie, Rose of Lima, Rose of Viterbo, Thérèse of Lisieux, and Victoria. The rose was depicted as a martyr's crown on statues and in early paintings, while Christian mystics associated the five petals of a red rose with the five wounds of Christ. Later, beautiful stained-glass rose windows were to adorn the great cathedrals of Europe.

*S*t. Elizabeth of Hungary (1207-34) was betrothed at the age of four and married at fourteen to the Landgrave of Thuringia. From an early age she was concerned with the welfare of the poor but when her husband died, she was driven from her home and forbidden to carry on with her merciful works. A charming legend tells how, one day, when smuggling bread in her apron to feed the hungry, she was stopped and ordered to show what she was hiding. When she opened her apron it was, miraculously, full of roses.

*I*n the Christian calendar, the fourth Sunday in Lent is Laetare Sunday, or Rose Sunday, when the Pope blesses The Golden Rose, an ornament in the shape of a spray of roses, one of which contains a receptacle for balsam and musk. It is bestowed occasionally on sovereigns and distinguished persons.

*T*he devotions of the rosary supposedly began with St. Dominic in the 13th century, and it is thought that rose hips, or pressed rose petals, were used as the first rosary beads. In about 1467, one of St. Dominic's followers, a monk named Francesco Collona, wrote an allegorical romance, *The Hyperotomachia Poliphili,* which gave details of garden design. An illustrated edition of 1499 showed a garden planted with roses that were known and named by Pliny. The garden was surrounded by pots and vases containing plants, such as boxwood *(Buxus),* lavender cotton *(Santolina chamaecyparissus),* marjoram *(Oreganum majorana),* and myrtle *(Myrtus),* which are still seen in rose gardens today.

A rose was frequently depicted in heraldry, and was the mark of cadency of a seventh son. Many English kings and nobles chose a rose for their emblem. In 1465 a new coin, the *Rose Noble*, which had a rose on its reverse side, was minted. It was revived in turn by Henry VII, Mary Tudor, and Elizabeth I. James I issued a similar coin, a rose-royal, during his reign.

*T*he 15th-century Wars of the Roses in England came about as a result of a period of weak government, which resulted in a dispute between the houses of Lancaster and York over the succession to the English throne. Supposedly, in a scene imaginatively described by Shakespeare, the Lancastrians chose a red rose, probably *R. gallica* var. *officinalis*, for their badge, while the Yorkists chose a white rose, possibly *R.* 'Alba Maxima'. The fortunes of the two houses waxed and waned over thirty years, but eventually the Lancastrian claimant was victorious at the battle of Bosworth Field, became Henry VII, and married Elizabeth of York. The two badges were combined in the red and white Tudor rose *(R. damascena* var. *versicolor)*, as a sign of national unity.

*I*n 1519, when the Spanish explorer, Cortés, entered the Aztec capital, Tenochtitlán, where Mexico City now stands, he was astonished by its beauty, and *"...never tired of looking at the diversity of the trees, and noting the scent which each one had, and the paths full of roses and flowers."* In other cities, the Aztecs hung their houses and streets with festoons of honeysuckle *(Lonicera)* and roses, gave bunches of roses to the soldiers, and hung rose wreaths on the invaders' helmets.

*I*n 16th-century New Mexico, the Spanish built many courtyards in which they grew plants, including lavender *(Lavandula)*, lilies, pinks *(Dianthus)*, and musk and Castillian roses, which they had brought from Spain. English colonists who arrived in Virginia in 1607, and the others who followed them from many parts of the Old World, also brought plants, roots, and seeds with them.

A 15th-century illustration depicts a double rose, as did the two, hinged, painted panels of the famous Wilton Diptych, of around 1395. A very beautiful set of tapestries, known as *The Hunting of the Unicorn*, of the type called millefleurs, hangs in the Cloisters Museum in New York. Made in about 1500, it depicts more than 100 flowers, including forget-me-nots *(Myosotis)*, pansies and violets *(Viola)*, primroses *(Primula)*, centifolia roses, and wallflowers *(Cheiranthus)*, all growing in the renowned flowery meadows of the period.

The rose became a little less fashionable, in Europe at least, during the late 17th and early 18th centuries, although it always had its admirers.

In Holland, however, the Dutch breeders were at work, and it is from them that we have the hybrid centifolia roses. Fortunately for us, the old roses lingered on, and we must be grateful to the Empress Josephine (1763-1814), wife of Napoleon, who made a great garden at Malmaison, in France, where she not only grew a vast collection of old roses, but also encouraged breeders to develop new varieties.

*I*n late-Victorian and Edwardian times, the rose garden achieved new status. Many enthusiastic amateurs grew roses, and some wrote knowledgeably on the subject. Since then, roses have never been out of fashion, claiming thousands of new devotees every year, all over the world. Breeders, including some gifted amateurs, constantly produce new varieties to delight us. Beautiful as many of these new roses are, however, it seems unlikely that they will ever oust the old, well-loved favorites. The 20th century has witnessed a great revival of interest in these lovely, fragrant old roses that inspire devotion in all who see them.

"Roses — nothing can be more favourable than to dream of these beautiful flowers, as they are certain emblems of happiness, prosperity and long life."

From *A Victorian Book of Dreams*.

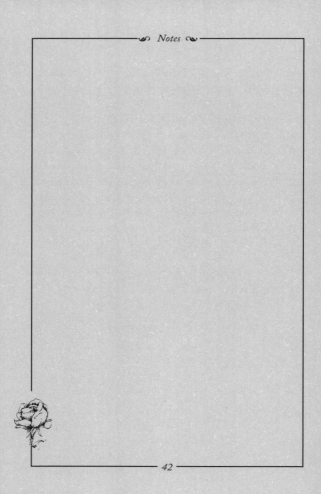

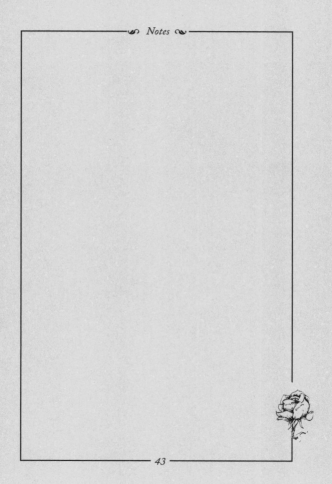

CHAPTER TWO

The Rose Family

*"The Ancient roses
Great families of yesterday we show,
And lords, whose parents are, the Lord knows who."*

Daniel Defoe

*A*ll the roses in cultivation today are descended from wild roses, and many roses cultivated and described by the ancient writers still grow in our gardens today. From graceful climbers, foaming with blossoms, down to the charming miniatures, there is a rose for everyone. Some flower in one great flush in spring or early summer, others produce a second flush, while many bloom, with varying degrees of generosity over a long period, and may produce a few flowers in midwinter. *R. rugosa,* *R. wichuraiana*, and *R. pimpinellifolia* are often used to breed hybrids that will withstand the winters in the colder parts of Canada and the United States. Most roses are hardy in the United Kingdom, although some, such as the sempervirens ramblers, which are descended from the wild rose *R. sempervirens,* and others descended from some Chinese roses, may not survive in the colder parts of the country, unless they are grown in a sheltered position and given winter protection. If you are not sure if a particular rose is hardy enough for your area, consult the supplier, your garden center, or the local rose society.

Flower Shapes

Blooms vary greatly in shape and in number of petals.

Flat: Single which has 4-7 petals, or semidouble which has 8-14 petals.

Cupped: Open shape, with petals curving away from the center; single to fully double, has 15-20 petals.

Pointed: High center, with tightly furled petals; semidouble to fully double, with more than 30 petals.

Urn-shaped: Curved, with a slightly flat top; semidouble to double (8-20 petals).

Globular: Double, with the many petals closing in to form a tight ball.

FLAT

CUPPED

POINTED

URN

Rounded: Double or fully double, with overlapping petals.

Rosette: Low-centered, slightly flat, double or fully double, with short petals.

Quartered: Slightly flat, semidouble or fully double, with inner petals in four sections.

Pompon: Small, rounded, double or fully double, with many short petals.

ROUNDED   **ROSETTE**

QUARTERED   **POMPON**

Petal Shapes

Plain: Flat or slightly curved.

Reflexed: Tips curl over and under.

Ruffled: Edges slightly crimped.

Frilled: Edges serrated.

Foliage

Rose foliage is often attractive—it may be deciduous, evergreen, or semievergreen; glossy, semiglossy, matte, or rugose (veined and wrinkled). Colors range through all shades of green. Several, *R. filipes,* for example, have grayish foliage, and on others, such as *R. glauca,* it is bluish. *R. virginiana* and some others color magnificently in autumn, and a few, such as *R. eglanteria,* have fragrant foliage. Others have delicate, fernlike leaves, or young shoots that are pink, bronze, or bloodred. The stems and moss of a few old garden roses are fragrant when crushed, and *R. sericea pteracantha* has large, flat, rubyred thorns, which are quite spectacular when the sun shines through them.

Colors

You will find roses in almost any color, or combination of colors, you can think of—all shades of pink, from blush to cerise; dusky red or brave scarlet; purple or lavender; white, pale cream, or gold; orange or copper—there are even green and brown ones. Some are a single color, others are bicolored, multicolored, or striped, or have buds of one color and blooms of another. Only a truly blue rose still eludes the breeders.

Fragrance

Fragrance is the greatest glory of the rose. In some, it is strong, in others, elusive. Not everyone agrees on which roses have fragrance or which smell of what—scents of apple, cinnamon, cloves, lemon, lilac, orange, musk, myrrh, peony, raspberry, sweetpea, tea, and violet have all been identified by different people.

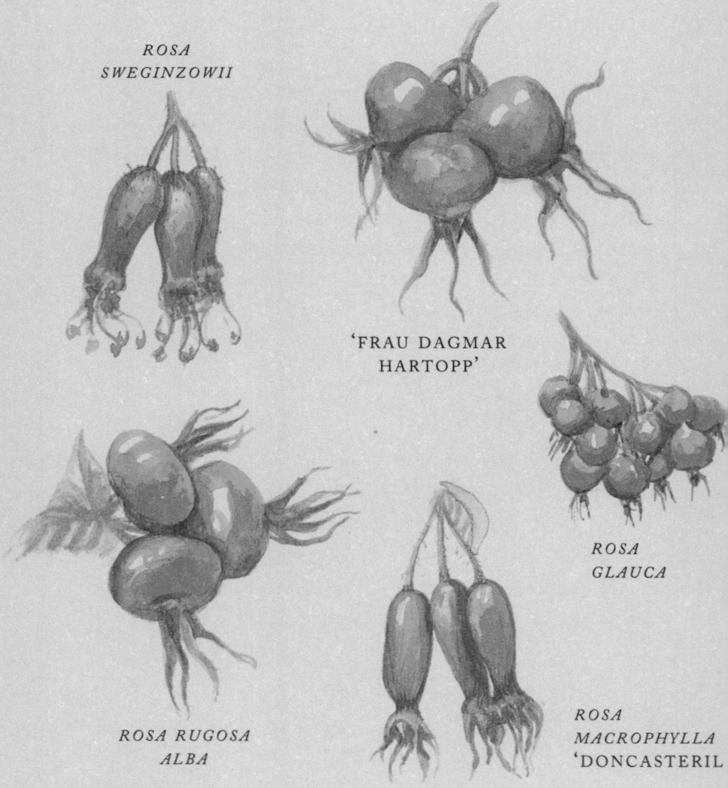

ROSA
SWEGINZOWII

'FRAU DAGMAR
HARTOPP'

ROSA
GLAUCA

ROSA RUGOSA
ALBA

ROSA
MACROPHYLLA
'DONCASTERIL

Hips

Roses that bear attractive hips should not be deadheaded, but left to form their beautiful fruits, which
may be yellow, orange, many shades of red, or even
black. The hips of some roses are small, glossy, and
borne in clusters, while on others, such as
'Madame Grégoire Staechelin' and many
rugosas, they are large and globular. The
hips produced by *R. moyesii* are flask-
shaped, while those of *R. roxburghii*
and *R. davidii* are prickly.

*ROSA
SCHARLACHGLUT*

'RUBRICAULIS'

'ST.
NICHOLAS'

Climbers and Ramblers

*T*hese constitute a large group of roses, all of which you can train to climb up arbors, arches, fences, pavilions, pergolas, trellises, tunnels, and walls, around pillars, posts, ropes, or chains.

Larger specimens look wonderful growing through and over shrubs and trees. Some climbers and ramblers can be pegged down as groundcovers or trained to disguise old tree stumps or manhole covers. Those with more flexible stems will trail as readily as climb, and look charming if you grow them to cascade over banks or the retaining walls of terraces. You can extend the floral display by growing climbing and rambling roses with other vines, and planting evergreen, silver-leaved plants around them to hide their bare stems.

Climbers

Climbers have stiff canes and large flowers. They may be recurrent (repeat flowering) or nonrecurrent (single flush).

'ALTISSIMO'
Height: 10-12ft (3-3.6m)
Color: Red, with gold stamens
Flowers: Large, single, flat, slightly fragrant
Flowering period: All season
Foliage: Dark green
Health: Disease-resistant
❧ A stunning rose, useful on walls, trellises, and posts.

'COMPASSION'
Height: 8-10ft (2.4-3m)
Color: Apricot pink
Flowers: Large, double, hybrid tea (HT) shape, very fragrant
Flowering period: All season
Foliage: Large, glossy
Health: Disease-resistant
❧ A good rose for a pillar or wall

'LAWRENCE JOHNSTON'
Height: 20ft (6m)
Color: Yellow
Flowers: Large, semi-double, in trusses, fragrant
Flowering period: Early summer
Foliage: Glossy
Health: Can be susceptible to black spot
❧ A good rose for covering a large area

'MADAME ALFRED CARRIÈRE'
Height: 10-15ft (3-4.5m)
Color: White
Flowers: Large, double, globular, fragrant
Flowering period: Recurrent
Foliage: Light green
Health: Disease-resistant
❧ A charming noisette climber, at its best on a wall

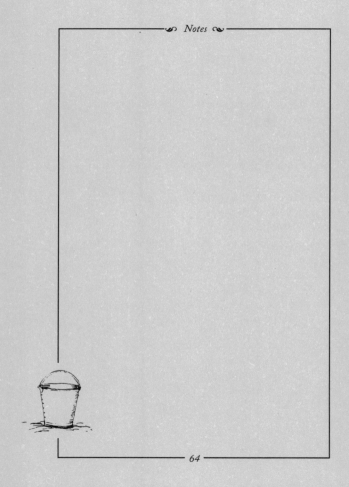

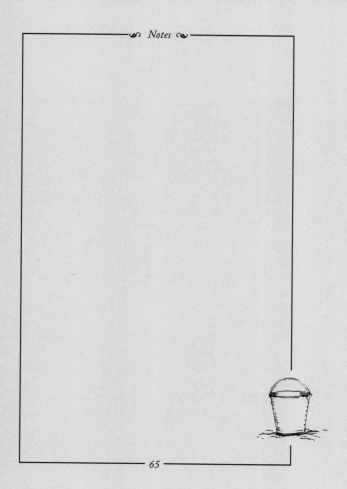

Ramblers

Ramblers have long, supple canes that carry trusses of small flowers in summer.

'ALBÉRIC BARBIER'
Height: 16ft (4.8m)
Color: Cream
Flowers: Medium-sized, double, with loosely muddled petals, slightly apple-scented.
Flowering period: Midsummer
Foliage: Dark green, glossy, semi-evergreen
Health: Disease-resistant
❧ At its best growing on a pillar

'ALBERTINE'
Height: 16ft (4.8m)
Color: Salmon pink
Flowers: Medium-large, double, fragrant
Flowering period: Midsummer
Foliage: Dark green
Health: Can be susceptible to mildew
❧ Very vigorous; excellent for large walls and trees

'BOBBIE JAMES'
Height: 26ft (7.8m)
Color: White
Flowers: Smallish, semidouble, in trusses, fragrant
Flowering period: Midsummer.
Foliage: Green with copper tints
Health: Disease-resistant
∾ A wonderful, rampant rose with prickly canes; it needs plenty of space and is excellent growing through a tree

'CRIMSON SHOWER'
Height: 9ft (2.7m)
Color: Crimson, with gold stamens
Flowers: Small rosettes in clusters, slightly fragrant
Flowering period: Late summer
Foliage: Pale green
Health: Disease-resistant
∾ Makes a good weeping tree rose (standard) or can be pegged down as groundcover

'DOROTHY PERKINS'
Height: 10-12ft (3-3.6m)
Color: Pink
Flowers: Small pompons in sprays, no fragrance
Flowering period: One generous flowering after mid-summer
Foliage: Medium green
Health: Can be susceptible to mildew
so An old favorite; best on arches and pergolas

'EMILY GRAY'
Height: 14ft (4.2m)
Color: Yellow, with gold stamens
Flowers: Small, semidouble, loosely cupped, fragrant
Flowering period: Midsummer
Foliage: Dark green, glossy, almost evergreen, richly tinted bronze when young
Health: Disease-resistant
so Excellent on walls and trellises

'VEILCHENBLAU'
Height: 15ft (4.5m)
Color: Violet-blue
Flowers: Small, semidouble, cupped, in clusters, fragrant
Flowering period: Midsummer
Foliage: Light green
Health: Disease-resistant
❧ An unusual rose, good against a wall, if shaded from the noon-day sun

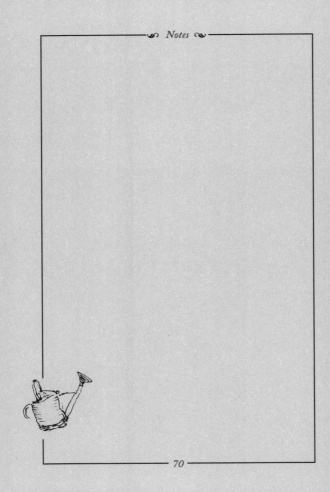

Floribundas

*I*mmensely popular roses that are ideal in many situations, floribundas are usually healthy, free-flowering over a long season, and fragrant. Early this century, rose-breeders began crossing hybrid teas with polyantha roses to obtain large, well-shaped flowers over a long season. The Danish breeder D.T. Poulsen produced the first hybrid polyantha roses, whose name was changed to floribundas. They are excellent for bedding, mixed borders, hedges, and containers, and many can be grown as tree roses. Those with single or semidouble blooms look particularly attractive in mixed borders and informal planting schemes.

'DUSKY MAIDEN'
Height: 2-3ft (60-90cm)
Color: Red, with gold stamens
Flowers: Medium-sized, single, saucer-shaped, fragrant
Flowering period: Midseason, with repeat
Foliage: Dark green
Health: Disease-resistant
ↄ A beautiful, upright, shapely rose

'HARVEST FAYRE'
Height: 2¹/₂ft (75cm)
Color: Apricot orange
Flowers: Medium-sized, double, hybrid tea shape, slightly fragrant
Flowering period: Late summer and fall
Foliage: Medium green, glossy
Health: Disease-resistant
ↄ A strong, well-shaped bush, with abundant foliage; later to flower than most

'LAVENDER PINOCCHIO'
Height: 2-3ft (60-90cm)
Color: Lavender
Flowers: Medium-sized, double, loosely ruffled, fragrant
Flowering period: Midseason, with repeats

Foliage: Midgreen, leathery
Health: Disease-resistant
❧ A delightful, most unusual rose; strong, bushy, and compact; good in a container or as a small hedge

'MARGARET MERRIL'
Height: 3-4ft (90-120cm)
Color: White
Flowers: Medium-sized, double, shapely, slightly ruffled, very fragrant
Flowering period: Long
Foliage: Midgreen, slightly glossy
Health: Disease-resistant
❧ One of the most sweetly scented modern roses

'PRINCESS ALICE'
Height: 3$^1/_2$-5ft (105-150cm)
Color: Yellow, tipped with red in hot weather
Flowers: Medium-sized, double, cupped, slightly ruffled, fragrant
Flowering period: Late season, with regular repeats
Foliage: Medium green, semiglossy
Health: Disease-resistant
❧ A slim, upright, vigorous rose; good wherever a narrow shape is needed

'PURPLE TIGER'
Height: 1¹/₂-2ft (45-60cm)
Color: Deep purple, flecked and striped with white, pink, or mauve
Flowers: Medium-large, double, flattish, slightly fragrant
Flowering period: Long
Foliage: Midgreen, glossy
Health: Can be susceptible to black spot and mildew.
᠘ A well-shaped, compact, bushy little rose

'SEXY REXY'
Height: 3-4ft (90-120cm)
Color: Pink
Flowers: Medium-sized, double, camellia-shaped, slightly fragrant
Flowering period: Midseason, with repeat
Foliage: Dark green, glossy
Health: Disease-resistant
᠘ An upright, shapely bush, one of the best pink floribundas; deadhead regularly to maintain flowering

Hybrid Teas

A large, and ever-popular group, the first hybrid tea rose is believed to be 'La France'. The result of a cross between a hybrid perpetual and a tea rose, it was introduced in France in 1867, although some work had been done before that. In general, the long, furled bud opens to a lovely, well-formed head with reflexing petals that loosen and soften charmingly as the rose ages. Though not as free-flowering as the floribundas, if well-tended, and deadheaded they flower on-and-off throughout the summer. They do best in beds by themselves, except, perhaps, for some low underplanting and small bulbs. Small, evergreen hedges around the rose beds add interest when the bushes are bare. They make excellent cut flowers.

'ELINA'
Height: 5ft (1.5m)
Color: Soft yellow
Flowers: Large, double,
high-centered, slightly
fragrant
Flowering period:
Very long
Foliage: Dark green,
semiglossy
Health: Disease-resistant
❧ A tall, bushy, and vigorous rose

'INGRID BERGMAN'
Height: 4ft (1.2m)
Color: Red
Flowers: Large, double, high-
centered, slightly fragrant
Flowering period: All season
Foliage: Dark green,
semiglossy
Health: Disease-resistant
❧ Good for flower
arrangements

'JUST JOEY'
Height: 3-4ft (90-120cm)
Color: Orange-apricot
Flowers: Large, double, high-centered, ruffled, very fragrant
Flowering period: All season
Foliage: Dark green, matte
Health: Disease-resistant
∾ Voted the world's favorite rose in 1994

'PASCALI'
Height 3¹/₂-4ft (1-1.2m)
Color: Creamy white
Flowers: Medium-sized, double, classic hybrid tea shape, slightly fragrant
Flowering period: All season
Foliage: Midgreen, semiglossy
Health: Disease-resistant
∾ Rain-resistant blooms; a good rose for cutting

'PINK FAVORITE'
Height: 4-4¹/₂ft (1.2-1.4m)
Color: Pink
Flowers: Medium-large, double, loosely cupped, slightly fragrant

Flowering period: Profuse midseason flush, with good repeats
Foliage: Dark green, glossy
Health: Disease-resistant
∾ Excellent for bedding

'SUMMER DREAM'
Height: 4-5ft (1.2-1.5m)
Color: Apricot pink
Flowers: Large, double, classic hybrid tea shape, fragrant
Flowering period: Good midseason flush, with outstanding repeats
Foliage: Medium green, matte
Health: Disease-resistant
∾ A vigorous, upright, well-shaped, bushy rose

Miniatures

*T*he tiny rose *R. roulettii*, the ancestor of today's miniatures, was discovered by Dr. Roulet in 1918, growing in a pot on a windowsill in Switzerland. You can display these charming, surprisingly hardy little bushes in raised beds, low terraces, rockeries, troughs, and pots, or as hedges, edges, or miniature "tree" roses.

'EASTER MORNING'
Height: 12-16in (30-47cm)
Color: White
Flowers: Width 1½in (3.5cm), fully double, in clusters
Flowering period: Continuous
Foliage: Small, dark green, glossy
Health: Disease-resistant
∾ Good for edging the front of a border, in small spaces, or containers

'POMPON DE PARIS'
Height: 8-10in (20-25cm)
Color: Deep pink
Flowers: Width 1in (2.5cm), double, cupped, no fragrance
Flowering period: All season
Foliage: Glossy
Health: Disease-resistant
❧ A Victorian miniature, dating from 1839

'RISE 'N' SHINE'
Height: 10-14in (25-35cm)
Color: Yellow
Flowers: Width 1½-1¾in (3.5-4.5cm), double, classic hybrid tea shape, slightly fragrant
Flowering period: Midsummer, with good repeat
Foliage: Midgreen, matte
Health: Disease-resistant
❧ Color doesn't fade with age; an award-winning show variety

'STARINA'
Height: 12-16in (30-40cm)
Color: Vermilion
Flowers: Width 1³/₄in (4.5cm), double, classic hybrid tea shape, no fragrance
Flowering period: Midsummer, with good repeat
Foliage: Glossy
Health: Disease-resistant
❧ A vigorous, compact, upright, little bush

'STARS 'N' STRIPES'
Height: 10-14in (25-35cm)
Color: Crimson with white stripes
Flowers: Width 1³/₄in (4.5cm), semidouble, open-cupped, no fragrance
Flowering period: Midsummer, with good repeat
Foliage: Light-medium green
Health: Disease-resistant
❧ An upright, but spreading, little bush; good in borders and hanging baskets and on the show bench

Miniatures / Patio Roses

A fast-growing group of dwarf floribunda roses, miniatures are compact and bushy, with leaves and flowers to scale. Developed for today's small gardens ,they are everblooming, and ideal for beds, hedges, and containers, providing a splash of color wherever it is needed. They can also be grown as standards.

'ANNA FORD'
Height: 18in (45cm)
Color: Orange-red with yellow center
Flowers: Small, semi-double, slightly fragrant
Flowering period: Continuous
Foliage: Glossy
Health: Disease-resistant
⤫ Needs good soil, but will tolerate light shade

'CIDER CUP'
Height: 12in (30cm)
Color: Apricot
Flowers: Small, semidouble, hybrid tea shape, slightly fragrant
Flowering period: Long
Foliage: Medium green, glossy
Health: Disease-resistant
∾ Good in beds and containers, or as a small hedge; excellent for cutting

'KIM'
Height: 18in (45cm)
Color: Yellow, flushed with red in hot weather
Flowers: Medium-sized, double, hybrid tea shape, slightly
fragrant
Flowering period: Long
Foliage: Dark green, matte
Health: Disease-resistant
∾ Bushy and hardy; excellent for smaller gardens, in borders, and containers

'LAVENDER JEWEL'
Height: 12in (30cm)
Color: Lavender
Flowers: Medium-sized, double, hybrid tea shape, slightly
fragrant
Flowering period: Long
Foliage: Dark green, glossy
Health: Disease-resistant
❧ Compact, bushy growth; very effective in beds and containers

'PINK SYMPHONY' / 'PRETTY POLLY'
Height: 16in (40cm)
Color: Pink
Flowers: Small, fully double, cupped—opening flat, slightly fragrant
Flowering period: Long
Foliage: Medium green, glossy
Health: Disease-resistant
❧ Dense and free-flowering, tolerant of many

conditions; good in borders and containers

'RED RASCAL'
Height: 16in (40cm)
Color: Red
Flowers: Small, fully double, cupped, slightly fragrant
Flowering period: Recurrent
Foliage: Dark green, glossy
Health: Disease-resistant
❧ Neat, even growth; tolerant of soil and climate; good for small beds and containers, and as cut flowers

'TEAR DROPS'
Height: 16in (40cm)
Color: White, with gold stamens
Flowers: Small, semidouble, in rosettes, slightly fragrant
Flowering period: Long
Foliage: Light green, glossy
Health: Disease-resistant
❧ Good for edging a bed or border

*O*ld Garden Roses / Shrub Roses

*T*his group embraces many beautiful roses of all sizes and colors. They are suitable for a wide range of situations and soils.

Albas

*B*eautiful, vigorous roses with *R. canina* in their ancestry. They are strong, upright, and often arching. Their fragrant, white or pink blooms appear in one glorious midsummer flowering. Albas will tolerate light shade.

'CELESTIAL' / 'CÉLESTE'
Height: 5ft (1.5m)
Color: Pink with red stamens
Flowers: Large, semidouble, camellia-shaped, fragrant
Flowering period: Midsummer
Foliage: Gray-green
Health: Disease-resistant
❧ Excellent for hedging or as a specimen

'MADAME LEGRAS DE SAINT GERMAIN'
Height: 7ft (2.1m)
Color: White with lemon center
Flowers: Large, fully double, cupped, petals reflexed when open, fragrant
Flowering period: Early summer
Foliage: Gray-green
Health: Disease-resistant

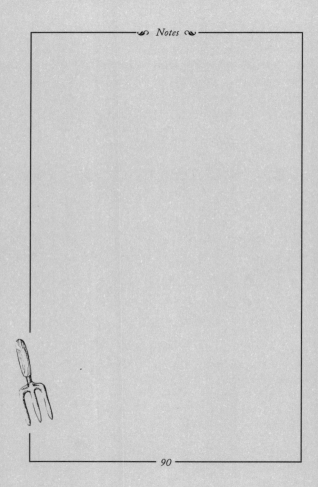

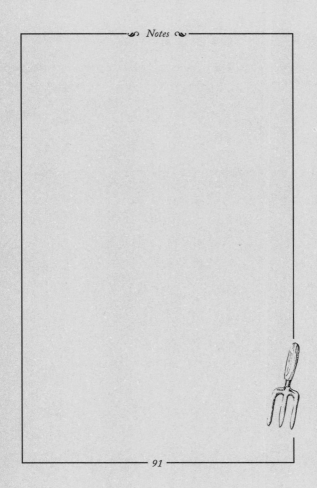

Bourbons

A seedling was found by chance in 1817 on the Ile de Bourbon (Reunion), and its seeds were sent to Paris. From these developed a large group of roses, diverse in size and color. Bourbons have glossy foliage that is often red-tinted.

'Boule de Neige'
Height: 5ft (1.5m.)
Color: Crimson buds, white flowers
Flowers: Medium-sized, globular, fragrant
Flowering period: Midsummer, with repeat.
Foliage: Dark green
Health: Disease-resistant
∽ A slender, upright rose

'Madame Isaac Periere'
Height: 5ft (1.5m)
Color: Crimson-purple
Flowers: Huge, double, quartered, very fragrant
Flowering period: Recurrent
Foliage: Medium green
Health: Can be susceptible to mildew

Centifolias

Centifolias are medium-sized, graceful shrubs with large, tightly packed flowers that appear once in summer. The shrubs will tolerate a little light shade, and respond well to pruning. Many centifolias were hybridized by Dutch breeders between the 16th and the 18th centuries.

'PETITE DE HOLLAND'
Height: 3$^{1}/_{2}$-4ft (105-120cm)
Color: Clear pink with deep pink center
Flowers: Small, full, globular, fragrant
Flowering period: Midseason
Foliage: Small, midgreen
Health: Disease-resistant
∽ A neat, slim, upright rose with thorny canes

'ROBERT LE DIABLE'
Height: 4ft (1.2m)
Color: Crimson, pink, purple, or slate
Flowers: Medium-large, fully double, fragrant
Flowering period: Late summer
Foliage: Midgreen abundant
Health: Not disease-resistant

China Roses

Cultivated in China from early times, there is some uncertainty about when these roses arrived in Europe, but it is possible they were taken there by explorers in the 17th century. Their recurrent bloom transformed European roses. The flowers darken with age and fall promptly. In favored regions, they have a long flowering season. They are delightful bedding roses and, although not winter hardy, small specimens will flower under glass or indoors in colder areas.

'ARCHDUKE CHARLES'
Height: 2-3ft (60-90cm)
Color: Blended pink, red, and white; color deepens with age and hot weather
Flowers: Medium-sized, double, beautifully shaped, very fragrant
Flowering period: Recurrent
Foliage: Light green, glossy
Health: Disease-resistant
ﻌ A moderately vigorous, bushy, and free-flowering rose; likes sun and a humus-rich soil

Damasks

Richly perfumed roses with downy, gray-green foliage, most damasks flower once, over a longish period, and repay good soil and pruning. Their dried petals retain their scent, and are used in herbal medicine and for attar of roses and potpourri.

'GLOIRE DE GUILAN'
Height: 5ft (1.5m)
Color: Pink
Flowers: Large, double, quartered, very fragrant
Flowering period: Early to midsummer
Foliage: Light green
Health: Disease-resistant
❧ A sprawling, prickly, free-flowering rose.

'LEDA'
Height: 3ft (90cm)
Color: Red buds, white petals with "painted" red edges
Flowers: Medium-sized, double, fragrant
Flowering period: Midsummer
Foliage: Gray-green
Health: Disease-resistant

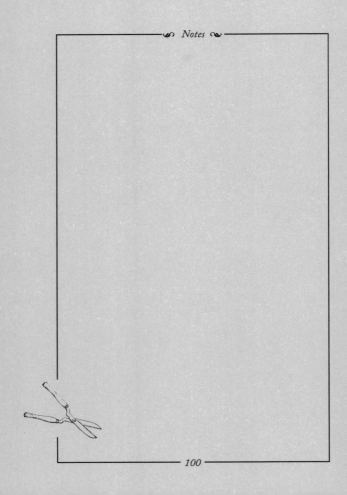

Eglanterias / Sweet Briars

*T*hese are vigorous, thorny shrubs that make good barrier hedges. Most have scented foliage. The Penzance Briars were first developed by Lord Penzance in the 19th century.

EGLANTINE / *R. RUBIGINOSA*
Height: 9ft (2.7m)
Color: Pale pink, followed by oval, red hips
Flowers: Small, single, flattish, five petals, fragrant
Flowering period: Early summer
Foliage: Apple-scented when wet
Health: Disease-resistant
᪶ Tolerates light shade and poor soil; upright and vigorous, it makes a good, prickly hedge

'HEBE'S LIP'
Height: 4ft (1.2m)
Color: White with red edge and yellow stamens, followed by ornamental hips
Flowers: Medium-sized, semidouble, flattish, fragrant
Flowering period: Early summer
Foliage: Gray-green

Gallicas

*V*igorous, nonrecurrent roses with prickly stems. The flowers come in all shades of pink, purple, and maroon, and many are striped. The dried petals retain their scent.

'APOTHECARY'S ROSE' / *R. GALLICA* VAR. *OFFICINALIS*
Height: 5ft (1.5m)
Color: Reddish-pink with gold stamens, followed by round, red hips
Flowers: Medium-sized, semidouble, cupped, fragrant
Flowering period: Midsummer
Foliage: Medium green
Health: Disease-resistant
꙰ Possibly the oldest rose in cultivation; good in potpourri, and for culinary and medicinal use

'DUCHESSE DE MONTEBELLO'
Height: 5ft (1.5m)
Color: Blush pink
Flowers: Medium-sized, fully double, globular, fragrant
Flowering period: Midsummer
Foliage: Light green
Health: Disease-resistant

❧ A lax shrub, good grown as a specimen, or for informal hedging; will tolerate poor soil and light shade

'ROSA MUNDI' / *R. GALLICA* VAR. *VERSICOLOR*
Height: 3¹/₂ft (1m).
Color: Striped red, pink, and white, followed by red hips
Flowers: Medium-sized, semi-double, cupped, fragrant
Flowering period: Midsummer
Foliage: Medium green
Health: Can be
susceptible to mildew
❧ An ancient rose
with historical
connections; good
grown in a group
or for hedging

Hybrid Perpetuals

Evolved from Noisette, Bourbon, perpetual damask, and China roses, these are sometimes described as the bridge between old and new roses. They are recurrent and make good cut flowers.

'FRAU KARL DRUSCHKI'
Height: 5ft (1.5m)
Color: Pink buds, white flowers
Flowers: Large, double, HT shape, with high center, no fragrance
Flowering period: Recurrent
Foliage: Medium green
Health: Can be susceptible to mildew
∾ Soil tolerant, but does not do well in rain

'PAUL NEYRON'
Height: 5ft (1.5m)
Color: Pink, flushed lilac
Flowers: Enormous, fully double, with ruffled petals
Flowering period: Midsummer, with good repeat
Foliage: Large, rich green
Health: Disease-resistant

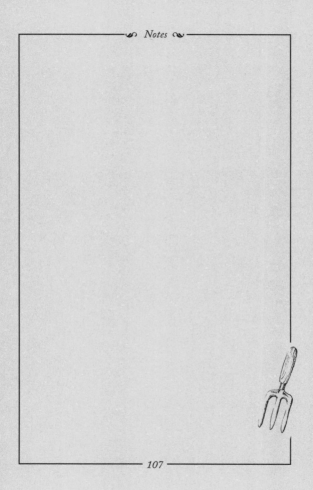

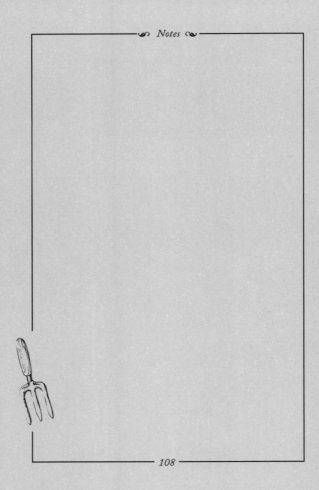

Hybrid Spinosissimas / Scots Roses

These roses were popular between 1790 and 1830, but few are still in cultivation. They are ferny, low-growing, and prickly, with musk-scented, well-shaped flowers. They do well in coastal gardens and on sandy soils, and are very hardy.

'FRÜHLINGSGOLD'
Height: 5-7ft (1.5-2.1m)
Color: Yellow, with gold stamens
Flowers: Large, single, flattish, fragrant
Flowering period: Early summer
Foliage: Light green
Health: Disease-resistant
❧ An excellent, modern spinosissima hybrid

'STANWELL PERPETUAL'
Height: 4ft (1.2m)
Color: Pale pink
Flowers: Medium-sized, double, rather frilly, fragrant
Flowering period: Recurrent
Foliage: Bluish green, ferny
Health: Disease-resistant

Moss Roses

These Victorian favorites have fragrant, double flowers and beautiful, mossy buds with long, ferny sepals. Both buds and stems are balsam-scented when crushed. Moss roses fall into two groups, both resulting from sports (mutations). One descends from the centifolias, the other from the damasks. The first recorded moss rose was *R. muscosa*, in 1768, which, except for its balsam-scented moss, was identical to *R. centifolia*.

'ALFRED DE DALMAS' /
'MOUSSELINE'
Height: 2-3ft (60-90cm)
Color: Light blush pink
Flowers: Medium-sized,
double, cupped, fragrant
Flowering period: Midsummer, with good repeat
Foliage: Fresh green
Health: Disease-resistant
❧ Bushy, upright, and spreading; good as a bedding rose or in a container

Noisettes

All Noisettes are descended from 'Champneys' Pink Cluster', a cross made between musk and China roses around 1802 by American planter and enthusiastic gardener John Champneys of Charleston, South Carolina. The two parent roses were sent to him by the brothers Noisette of France, who then developed many more varieties from the result of this first union. Noisettes have small to medium-sized, very fragrant flowers. They are not hardy.

'AIMÉE VIBERT'
Height: Up to 12ft (3.6m)
Color: Pure white
Flowers: Medium-sized, double, in small clusters, fragrant
Flowering period: Late summer, with a few repeats
Foliage: Dark green, narrow
Health: Disease-resistant

᠅ A vigorous, arching bush or climber. Tolerates poor soil and light shade, but flowers better in full sun.

Notes

Perpetual Damask / (Portland Roses)

A small group of charming roses perpetual damasks are descended from damask, gallica, and China roses. They were popular in the 19th century because of their repeat-flowering habit. They produce fragrant, fully double flowers on neat bushes, and respond well to rich soil, good drainage, and careful pruning. Not many varieties are still available.

'COMPTE DE CHAMBORD' / 'MADAME KNORR'
Height: 3-4ft (90-120cm)
Color: Pink
Flowers: Large, double, tightly packed, quartered, very fragrant
Flowering period: Midsummer, with good repeat
Foliage: Gray-green
Health: Disease-resistant
❧ Upright, compact, and moderately thorny; a good rose for bedding and hedging, especially in smaller gardens

'ROSE DU ROI'
Height: 3-4ft (90-120cm)
Color: Red
Flowers: Large, semidouble, very fragrant
Flowering period: Midsummer, with good repeat
Foliage: Medium-dark green, semiglossy
Health: Disease-resistant
ॐ An upright, compact, and vigorous rose

'ROSE DU ROI À FLEURS POURPRES'
Height: 3-4ft (90-120cm)
Color: Purple
Flowers: Large, semidouble, full, deep, very fragrant
Flowering period: Midsummer, with good repeat
Foliage: Medium-dark green, semiglossy
Health: Disease-resistant
ॐ Very similar to 'Rose du Roi'

Polyanthas / Shrubs

*T*hese are neat little recurrent shrub roses with small, often fragrant flowers borne in clusters. They are late to flower but continue until the first heavy frosts. They do well as hedges or in beds or containers, and make excellent tree roses.

'BABY FAURAX'
Height: 18in (45cm).
Color: Violet-pink with white centers and yellow stamens
Flowers: Small, double, in large clusters, no fragrance
Flowering period: Continuous
Foliage: Serrated
Health: Disease-resistant
ဆ A compact, bushy little rose; good at the front of a border, in a shallow terrace, or in a container

'THE FAIRY'
Height: 2ft (60cm)
Color: Pink
Flowers: Tiny, double pompons, in clusters, slightly fragrant
Flowering period: Late summer, with repeat
Foliage: Small, glossy
Health: Disease-resistant
෨ A prolific flowerer, with a bushy habit; excellent trained as a tree rose; good in beds, as a specimen, or for groundcover

'YVONNE RABIER'
Height: 2ft (60cm)
Color: White
Flowers: Small, double, well-shaped, fragrant
Flowering period: Recurrent
Foliage: Green, glossy
Health: Average disease-resistance
෨ Very free-flowering–a gem

Species Roses

*T*here are thought to be about 200 of these old, wild roses, most of which have great charm, and are very hardy. They are once-blooming, and the flowers of most are single and five-petaled. The shrubs are excellent grown either as specimens, or in groups toward the back of a large border. They are also ideal in woodland and informal settings.

R. X *HIGHDOWNENSIS*
Height: 9-12ft (2.7-3.6m)
Color: Red, followed by flask-shaped, orange hips
Flowers: Medium-sized, single, in clusters, slightly fragrant
Flowering period: Early summer
Foliage: Delicate, bluish
Health: Disease-resistant
❧ A beautiful rose with colorful thorns; will tolerate poor soil and some shade

Hybrid Musks

*I*n 1904, a German nurseryman marketed 'Trier', the forerunner of this delightful group of roses, which, despite the name, have very little musk in them, though many are fragrant. They tolerate some shade but flower better in sun.

'BALLERINA'
Height: 3-4ft (90-120cm)
Color: Pink with white eye
Flowers: Small, single, in large clusters, slightly fragrant
Flowering period: Midsummer
Foliage: Light green
Health: Disease-resistant
❧ A charming rose; excellent in a mixed border, in a group, or trained as a tree rose

'BUFF BEAUTY'
Height: 6ft (1.8m)
Color: Yellow, gold, and apricot
Flowers: Medium-sized, fully double, globular, fragrant
Flowering period: Midsummer, with good repeat
Foliage: Green, with purple tints
Health: Disease-resistant
❧ Arching and graceful, this is one of the loveliest roses

'CORNELIA'
Height: 5ft (1.5m)
Color: Coppery pink
Flowers: Small, double, rosette shape, fragrant
Flowering period: Midsummer through fall
Foliage: Tinted bronze
Health: Disease-resistant
❧ Good as a large specimen, or for hedging; particularly attractive in fall

Tea Roses

*B*rought from China, possibly in the tea-clippers of
the East India Company, tea roses range from dwarf
shrubs to tall climbers. They have a long flowering season and bear pointed buds that open to loosely cupped,
delicate, sweetly scented blooms. The stems are slim
and rather weak, and have few thorns. The foliage is
glossy. Most are not hardy. Tea roses were eventually
crossed with hybrid perpetuals to produce the hybrid
teas of today. A few of the old tea roses
are still available.

'LADY HILLINGDON'
Height: 2-3ft (60-90cm)
Color: Copper-apricot buds,
yellow-apricot flowers
Flowers: Medium-sized, double,
HT shape, very fragrant
Flowering period: Continuous
Foliage: Bronze
Health: Disease-resistant
❧ Upright and bushy, but
not vigorous; good in a container or under glass

Hybrid Rugosas

*R*ugosas are 20th-century hybrids of a species that was portrayed in Chinese paintings and illustrations in about AD 1000. Found in Korea, China, and Japan, it was taken to Europe by explorers and traders in the late 18th century. Vigorous and thorny, most have deeply veined, wrinkled leaves, charming, semidouble flowers, handsome hips, and drifting fragrance. They are tolerant of poor, sandy soils, but not so good on heavy clay or chalk. They need little pruning and are very hardy.

'BLANC DOUBLE DE COUBERT'
Height: 4-6ft (1.2-1.8m)
Color: White
Flowers: Medium-sized, semi-double, papery, very fragrant
Flowering period: Midsummer, with some repeats
Foliage: Medium green.
Health: Disease-resistant
∽ A wonderful rose, tolerant of some shade; good in a container or as a hedge

English Roses

This is a fast-growing group of roses that have been developed since the 1960s by English rose breeder David Austin. They combine the charming characteristics and fragrance of the old roses with the bushy, recurrent habit of the best modern varieties. Very useful and decorative, they are excellent grouped in beds or in mixed borders.

'Fair Bianca'
Height: 2^{1}/$_{2}$-3ft (75-90cm)
Color: White
Flowers Medium-sized, fully double, quartered, fragrant
Flowering period: Midsummer, with good repeat
Foliage: Light green, semiglossy
Health: Disease-resistant

'FISHERMAN'S FRIEND'
Height: 3-4ft (90-120cm)
Color: Red
Flowers: Very large, fully double, cupped, very fragrant
Flowering period: Recurrent
Foliage: Dark green, semiglossy
Health: Can be susceptible to black spot
❧ A good rose for a bed, or a low hedge; can be grown in a container

'GRAHAM THOMAS'
Height: 5-7ft (1.5-2.1m)
Color: Yellow
Flowers: Medium-sized, double, loosely cupped, very fragrant
Flowering period: Early summer through late fall
Foliage: Light green, semiglossy
Health: Disease-resistant
❧ A slender, vigorous, and free-flowering rose; the flowers hold their shape well until they drop

'THE REEVE'
Height: 3-4ft (90-120cm)
Color: Deep pink
Flowers: Medium-sized, fully double, globular, very fragrant
Flowering period: Midsummer, with good repeat
Foliage: Reddish
Health: Disease-resistant
❧ A spreading rose with reddish canes; good cascading over a low wall

'WILLIAM SHAKESPEARE'
Height: 4ft (1.2m)
Color: Crimson-purple
Flowers: Medium-sized, fully double, in sprays, fragrant
Flowering period: Recurrent
Foliage: Dark green, semiglossy
Health: Disease-resistant
❧ An upright rose with red thorns and old-fashioned charm; suitable for a wide range of soils and conditions, but appreciates shelter from strong winds

Modern Shrubs

This is a large and diverse group of comparatively recently introduced roses that do not fit neatly into other categories.

'CARDINAL HUME'
Height: 4ft (1.2m)
Color: Purple
Flowers: Small-medium, double, cupped, very fragrant
Flowering period: Midsummer, with excellent repeat
Foliage: Varying shades of green, matte
Health: Disease-resistant
❧ A vigorous, spreading rose with small thorns; will tolerate poor soils

'CONSTANCE SPRY'
Height: 5-6ft (1.5-1.8m)
Color: Pink
Flowers: Large, double, globular, very fragrant
Flowering period: Midsummer
Foliage: Dark green, glossy
Health: Disease-resistant
❧ Upright, arching, moderately thorny canes; good as a climber; will tolerate poor soil and some shade

'GOLDEN WINGS'
Height: 5ft (1.5m)
Color: Yellow with gold stamens
Flowers: Large, single, flattish, fragrant
Flowering period: All season
Foliage: Light green
Health: Disease-resistant
∽ A stunning, prolific, well-shaped, upright rose

'LA SEVILLANA'
Height: 3ft (90cm)
Color: Scarlet
Flowers: Medium-sized, semidouble, slightly fragrant
Flowering period: Midsummer, with excellent repeat
Foliage: Dark green, tinted red
Health: Disease-resistant
∽ Good groundcover rose

'NEVADA'
Height: 6-8ft (1.8-2.4m)
Color: White, with yellow stamens
Flowers: Large, single, saucer-shaped, slightly fragrant
Flowering period: Midsummer, with good repeat
Foliage: Medium green
Health: Disease-resistant
❧ Upright and arching–a wonderful sight when in flower

Groundcover Roses

*T*hese are useful for covering steep banks, large patches of bare earth, old tree stumps, manhole covers, and other problem areas. They are excellent when planted beneath taller roses, and often make excellent weeping tree roses.

'ALBA MEIDILAND'
Spread: 6ft (1.8m)
Color: White
Flowers: Large, double, cupped, in sprays, no fragrance
Flowering period: Midsummer
Foliage: Medium green, glossy
Health: Disease-resistant
❧ A spreading rose that requires little maintenance

'FERDY'
Spread: 4ft (1.2m)
Color: Coral-pink
Flowers: Small, semidouble, open-cupped, in large clusters, no fragrance
Flowering period: Recurrent
Foliage: Light green
Health: Disease-resistant

'NORFOLK'
Spread: 2ft (60cm)
Color: Yellow
Flowers: Small, double, pompon, fragrant
Flowering period: Two flushes
Foliage: Dark green
Health: Disease-resistant
❧ Strong, spreading, and bushy; will tolerate poor soil

'RED BLANKET'
Spread: 4ft (1.2m)
Color: Red
Flowers: Medium-sized, semidouble, saucer-shaped, in clusters, slightly fragrant
Flowering period: Recurrent
Foliage: Dark green
Health: Can be susceptible to black spot
❧ Small, arching, and vigorous; will tolerate poor soil and some shade; good in a container

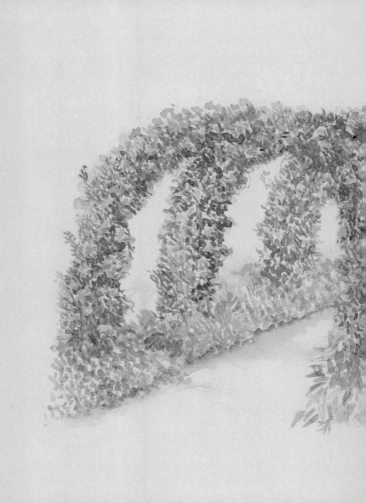

CHAPTER THREE
Roses in the Garden

"He who would have beautiful roses in his garden
must have beautiful roses in his heart."

Dean Hole

Roses are immensely versatile, and are agreeable in so many ways throughout the garden. On the porch and on the house or garden walls and fences, they can be seen in all their glory, relishing sheltered warmth in cooler areas and noon-time shade in hotter climates. From the tall, vigorous 'Mermaid', a glossy-leaved rose with large, single, yellow flowers, to the pink-flowered, fragrant 'Aloha', which grows to a mere 8ft (2.4m), there is a climbing or rambling rose for any wall.

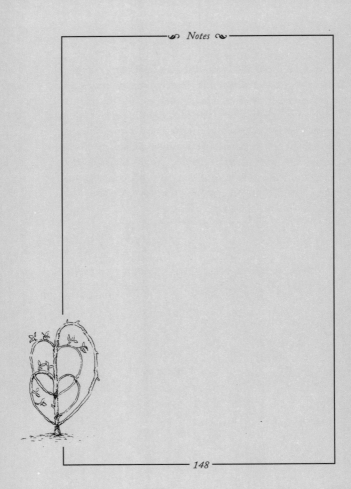

$\mathcal{A}$ lattice makes a practical and ornamental support for roses. Along the top of a low wall or fence, it provides privacy, and breaks the force of the wind, while allowing the free circulation of air. You can paint or stain latticework in a range of attractive colors, but don't use creosote because its fumes are toxic to plants. Walls can be covered completely with latticeworking or fitted with decorative panels. Use it for arches, arbors, tunnels, pyramids, and obelisks too, and for dividing up the garden. Make your own designs from strong timber lathes — flimsy lattice soon collapses. To cover arches and arbors, choose graceful climbers and ramblers, such as 'Adélaïde d'Orléans', which is semi-evergreen and vigorous, with sweetly scented, dangling blooms, or 'New Dawn', which has glossy, healthy foliage, and softly fragrant, blush pink flowers.

$\mathcal{M}$etal, sturdy wrought-iron, or delicate wirework makes decorative porches, arches, and tunnels. Ornamental pavilions, gazebos, bowers, arbors, and other secret hideaways, whether of metal or timber, are even more delightful when swathed in fragrant roses. Nothing is more pleasant than a sheltered seat in a shady, fragrant spot. Try the apple-scented, violet rambler 'Veilchenblau' or 'May Queen', a pink wichuraiana climber, bred from the wild rose *R. wichuraiana*. More simply, place slender hoops of iron along a path, both to display the roses and to invite the beholder onward. Alternatively, place a few slim metal obelisks in the borders where, clothed by short climbers and the more graceful shrub roses, they will enhance the overall design of the garden and add instant height to new or immature gardens. To prolong interest, add clematis in contrasting colors.

A well-made pergola, whether free-standing or built onto the house and garden walls, makes a handsome addition to any garden. When covered with scented roses and vines makes a delightful dining area in hot weather. Pergolas are usually made from stout, horizontal timbers supported by beams resting on uprights, which may be of timber, brick, or stone. You can also use iron poles, either on their own, or in conjunction with timber beams. Rustic pergolas made from larch poles look good in informal gardens. 'Albéric Barbier', with its cream, fragrant flowers, is a good rose for a pergola.

❧

*W*ooden or metal posts or pillars of stone or brick are especially useful when height is needed in borders and beds or in paved areas. As the roses grow, train them to twine around the supports, to help their flowering shoots to develop. Choose roses that grow to between 8ft (2.4m) and 15ft (4.5m). 'Buff Beauty', pink 'Bantry Bay', apricot 'Westerland', and the pink, thornless 'Zéphirine Drouhin' are all excellent. Chains and ropes strung between posts and pillars make elegant supports, tripods or little teepees of timber, branches, or twigs are delightful supports for less-vigorous roses in smaller gardens.

Notes

A traditional, formal rose garden has neat beds set in lawns, gravel, or paving, and is packed with tea roses and, nowadays, with hybrid tea and floribunda bushes, too. All the roses in the garden may be the same color, or a different color may be grown in each bed.

❧

*O*ld garden roses and shrub roses are best grown either as single specimens or in groups of three, five, or seven. They look spectacular in a formal lawn or in the wilder parts of informal and woodland gardens. Pink 'Marguerite Hilling' and the white 'Nevada' flower only once, but their attractive leaves and red canes make them interesting all year round.

❧

*M*iniatures will bring some welcome summer color to a rockery, where the main display of the other flowers is often in spring. Plant the roses among the lower-growing rock garden plants, where a little height will make a pleasing contrast. They will need to be watered regularly, and may have to be clipped over with scissors to keep them to an appropriate size.

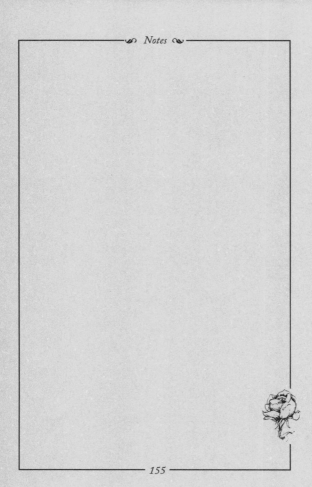

*F*loribundas, old garden roses, and shrub roses, old and new, can hold their own in company, and look better for it. Mixed borders of evergreen and silver-leaved shrubs, roses, herbaceous perennials, and bulbs are attractive all year long. These mixed plantings work very well in small to medium-sized gardens, where the bare twigs that stand alone in formal rose gardens for a large part of the year leave much to be desired. In a small garden, a central bed, either round, square, or diamond-shaped, makes a pleasant feature. Put a tree rose in the center, and underplant with pansies, alpine strawberries, lady's mantle *(Alchemilla mollis)*, or low-growing roses.

Rose hedges are beautiful in a garden. Plant rugosas, hybrid musks, and *R. gallica* var. *Versicolor* ('Rosa mundi'), for large, informal hedges. Where space is limited, neat polyantha and floribunda roses are best. Try the delightful polyantha 'Yvonne Rabier', which is white, free-flowering, and fragrant, to edge a path. The hardy, prickly, rugosas have the added advantages of scent, good fall color, and splendid hips, and make excellent barriers. If you want a narrow screen, choose tall, upright, hybrid teas or floribundas, such as 'Queen Elizabeth' or 'Anne Harkness'.

Hybrids musks, trained along wires,
trellises, or wooden frames, will
make a slim, flower-covered
screen or barrier to hide such
things as parking areas,
garbage cans, and wash
lines.

*T*ree roses provide a little instant height when it is needed, and make charming centerpieces in beds or small gardens. Half-sized and miniature tree roses are also available, and are particularly suitable for containers and small gardens. Many, such as 'The Fairy' and 'White Pet' bloom repeatedly but others, such as *R. xanthina* 'Canary Bird', are so generous in spring and have such attractive foliage that we can forgive their once-blooming habit. A border alongside a path looks charming with a row of tree roses underplanted with small floribundas or miniatures.

*F*ew things look as beautiful as a rose cascading from an old tree or smothering a dead one. Plant the rose on the tree's windward side, so that its long shoots will be blown toward the tree. Water copiously and mulch well in dry weather for the first year or two. Sink a 2ft (60cm) length of pipe into the ground beside the rose and fill it from a hosepipe to get water right down to the roots. Tie in new growth regularly to avoid wind damage. Vigorous and pliant 'Albèric Barbier', 'Climbing Cécile Brunner', coppery pink 'Albertine', *R. filipes* 'Kiftsgate', 'New Dawn', 'Paul's Himalayan Musk', 'Silver Moon', and 'Wedding Day' will envelop a tree, and perfume the whole garden. In protected areas, try *R. brunonii* 'La Mortola'.

Groundcover roses are perfect for covering a steep bank, and will suppress weeds at the same time. They need comparatively little maintenance and fall roughly into four main types: large, arching shrubs, such as 'Bonica', about 3½ft (1m) high by at least 5ft (1.5m) wide; smaller arching shrubs, such as 'Ferdy', up to 3ft (90cm) high by about 4ft (1.2m) wide; large, creeping shrubs, such as 'Weisse Immensee' / 'Partridge', upward of 18in (45cm) high by about 5ft (1.5m) wide; and small, creeping shrubs, no more than 18in (45cm) high and less than 5ft (1.5m) wide. 'Red Blanket' is a good example, and an excellent carpeter. 'Immensee' / 'Grouse' and the other wichuraiana hybrids hug the ground, rooting as they go, slowly covering quite large areas. *R. jacksonii* 'Max Graf', an older rose, is ideal for growing over a low wall or tree-stump, and 'Raubritter' is exceptionally hardy. The larger types will cover more bare ground, while the smaller ones, such as the white 'Swany', and the pink 'Avon', look good under taller roses, at the fronts of borders, and in containers.

*I*f you have no soil in which to plant, don't despair. Many roses, from climbers and ramblers down to the tiniest miniatures, grow well in containers, though larger specimens need sizeable ones if they are to thrive for any length of time. Roses in containers are perfect in yards and on patios, porches, windowsills, balconies, and roof terraces. One on each side of a door or at the top of a flight of steps is welcoming, and a double row will mark a path from one part of a paved garden to another. Window boxes and small troughs on balconies, low walls, porches, and narrow ledges, are perfect for miniature roses, as are hanging baskets and wall baskets. You can grow one of the shorter climbers or a pliant shrub in a tub, and train it over a porch, arch, pergola, or bench. Plant a row of roses in a large trough to cover walls, fences, or screens. Four or more troughs, set out in a square or rectangle, will make a secluded area for reclining or dining. Flexible climbing or rambling roses, and lax shrubs, planted in a trough or row of troughs set on top of a wall will trail prettily, and camouflage large, bare walls and ugly surfaces. A weeping tree rose in a large pot or tub makes a stunning centerpiece for a small courtyard. For emphasis, you can place potted roses on pillars, parapets, pedestals, and balustrades.

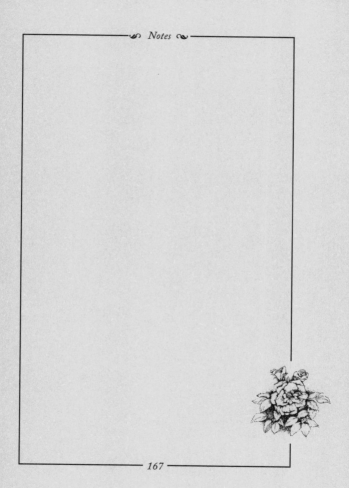

"*I know a little garden close,*
Set thick with lily and with rose,
Where I would wander if I might
From dewy dawn to dewy night."

William Morris

CHAPTER FOUR

The Cultivation of Roses

"There will I make thee beds of roses
And a thousand fragrant posies,
A cap of floweres, and a kirtle
Embroider'd all with leaves of myrtle."

Christopher Marlowe

Roses prefer moist, well-drained, fertile loams and open, sunny sites. They dislike deep shade, water-logged soil, strong winds, and overcrowded, poorly ventilated positions. With a little help, many will grow in sand, chalk, or heavy clay. A neutral to slightly acid soil suits them, and it is seldom necessary to add lime—if it is, add it sparingly. If your soil is a little too alkaline, amend it with sulfate of ammonia or spread a light mulch of lawn mowings (which must be free of herbicides), leaf mold, or composted green bracken. Roses appreciate light shade at noon, but don't plant them near trees or large shrubs, whose roots will compete for nutrients and water.

*T*ender roses grown against a sunny wall may survive cooler climates if they are given winter protection. Others, such as 'La Follette', a charming rose, raised at Cannes in 1910, will thrive in a conservatory. In some warmer regions, such as the southern states of America, tea roses and other frost-tender roses grow and flower freely in the open, but they have a very short period of dormancy and may become exhausted. In such areas, it may be advisable to leave the spent flowers on the roses from late fall to allow hips to form. This will create a state of semidormancy, which will rest the plants.

*I*n regions where winters are severe, a heavy covering of snow will give some protection, but in patchy snow or alternating periods of frosts and thaws, use polystyrene wrappings and cones or netting packed with newspapers, straw, or other insulating material. Alternatively, mound fresh soil over the crown, or the entire bush, before severe frosts begin. To bury tree roses, remove the soil from one side of the roots, bend the stem down into a trench that is long and deep enough to accommodate the whole plant, and cover it with slightly mounded soil. Mound fresh soil over the roots of climbers and ramblers, and protect the canes with insulating material, or, for long canes, dig a trench alongside the plant, peg down the canes, and bury them. Where severe frosts are rare, little winter protection is necessary—it is sufficient to prune long, whippy growth by a third, stake and tie the plants to prevent the bush being rocked by the wind, and firm the soil around their roots after frosty or windy weather.

Planting Pot-Grown Roses

*Y*ou can plant pot-grown roses any time except during prolonged dry spells or when the ground is frozen or waterlogged. If you can't plant them right away you can leave them in their pots for some weeks, provided you water them well and protect them from extremes of heat or cold. Choose bushy plants with healthy foliage, and avoid those without established root balls because the soil may fall away from the roots when you remove the pots. To test if the plant is well-rooted in the pot, grip the canes and shake gently–if the root ball is not well developed, the rose will shift loosely in the potting mix. Roots growing out from the bottom of the container usually mean that the plant is pot-bound–remove the pot and check that the roots are not coiled so tightly that it would be difficult to tease them out a little before planting.

*B*efore you begin to plant your roses, prepare a planting mix of equal parts of loam and peat substitute. To each 5 gallon (23 liter) bucketful of the mix add a handful of bonemeal. Dig a hole twice as wide and deep as the pot, and add some planting mix. Center the pot in this, so that the top of the soil in the pot is level with the surrounding soil.

*I*f the root ball is firm, slip the rose out of its pot, tease out a few roots and spread them in the hole, then fill with planting mix, firm well, and water. If the soil around the roots is loose, cut the base of the pot, supporting it on one hand, and make an upward cut halfway up each side of the pot. Stand the pot in the hole, slipping the base out as you go, then complete both cuts, and slide out the pot.

Planting Bareroot Roses

*I*n warm or temperate climates, plant bareroot roses while they are dormant and when the ground is neither frozen nor waterlogged. In colder regions, plant them in spring. If your soil is likely to be very wet in spring, cover it with sheets of plastic the previous fall.

*S*elect healthy plants with strong bud unions, good root systems, and two or three plump canes. Tree roses should have well-balanced heads on strong stems. Plant them as soon as possible. If delay is unavoidable, store them in their unopened packets in a cool, dark, frost-free place. Unwrapped roses need to be heeled in. Dig a trench not less than 1ft (30cm) deep, pack in the roses at an angle of 45°, and cover the roots with moist soil. Water them in dry weather and, if severe frosts are expected, mound them up with dead leaves or other insulating material and cover them with plastic. Remove the covering when the temperature rises above freezing.

*I*f the soil is very dry, soak it thoroughly some days before planting. Dig a hole for each rose, wide enough to accommodate the roots when they are spread out, and deep enough to leave the bud union 1in (2.5cm) below ground level when the soil is firmed. In colder regions, plant a little deeper.

*P*repare a planting mix, then unwrap the roses and stand them in water to which you have added a dash of liquid fertilizer. If the canes are shriveled, leave them in the water overnight. Immediately before planting, remove any leaves, flower heads, buds, and hips, and cut off any dead wood and damaged or weak twigs and shoots. Trim the roots, cutting thick ones back by one third, and damaged ones to just above the affected parts.

*M*ound some planting mix in the hole, then position the rose on the mound, spreading out the roots. Lay a stick across the hole to ensure the bud-union is at the correct level, and adjust if necessary. Fill the hole with more planting mix, shaking the rose gently so the soil trickles down among the roots, and firming as you work so that no pockets of air remain. Tread in, gently on heavy soils, a little more firmly on light soils, and water well.

*P*lant climbers and ramblers in the same way, but dig the holes at least 18in (45cm) away from the wall or fence. Trim as before, leaving the main canes unshortened. Spread the roots away from the wall or fence before refilling the hole, then firm down and water well. Train the canes toward the wall or fence by tying them to sticks leaning at an angle of 45°. Train growing shoots horizontally on wires or trellis or tied to wall nails. To plant at the foot of a tree, prepare the ground and the planting mix in the same way. Dig a good-sized hole at least 3ft (90cm) from the trunk. Position the rose to lean toward the tree at an angle of 45°. Train the shoots toward the tree by tying them to sticks.

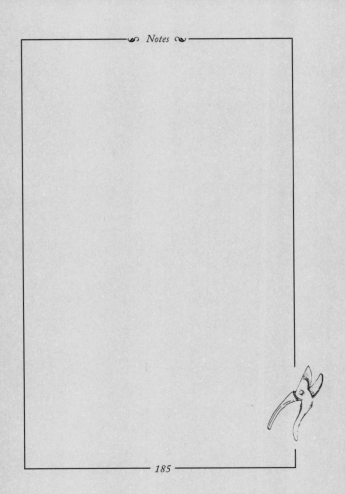

$\mathcal{A}$ll roses respond generously to regular care. Watch out for pest infestations, diseases, and failure to thrive, and take appropriate preventive or remedial action. Feed after spring pruning, when the soil is moist and warm, and again when the first blooms have finished. On light, sandy, or chalky soils, more frequent feeding is beneficial. Apply a foliar feed every two to three weeks from when the leaves appear, but stop soon after midsummer to discourage new, frost-susceptible growth. Depending on the size of the roses, after weeding and feeding, spread a 3-8in (7.5-20cm) layer of mulch to suppress weeds, conserve moisture, maintain soil temperature, and improve soil structure—well-rotted compost, manure, or bark chips are ideal.

$\mathcal{R}$emove annual weeds by hand or by shallow hoeing. Dig out perennial weeds or apply a contact weedkiller. Old gardeners say a green manure of turnips rids a bed of couch grass, so if this pernicious weed is a problem in your garden, it may be worth trying.

Pruning

Wear gloves when pruning, deadheading, or removing suckers. Deadhead regularly to encourage new flowers. Many roses produce suckers–these are strong, frequently prickly shoots, often of a different shade of green, and with different leaves and thorns, that grow from the original rootstock below the bud union, especially if the rootstock is damaged. Trace the suckers back to base, remove the soil gently to avoid further damage, then snap off the suckers (don't cut them off, as this encourages more to grow). On tree roses, snap suckers off cleanly, taking care not to tear the bark, or cut them off with a sharp pruning knife.

Pruning keeps plants shapely and stimulates strong new growth. Work on mild, frost-free days after leaf-fall, when the roses are dormant, or semidormant, between late fall and early spring, when the buds begin to break. In colder areas, prune in spring, cutting frost-damaged shoots back to healthy buds.

*L*ightly prune all roses to remove everything dead, damaged, or diseased, cutting back to healthy wood with a white pith. Remove shoots that cross or rub, and trim weak, spindly growth to "open up" the rose. Always cut above an outward-facing bud, sloping the cut down and away from it.

"*Jasmine is all in white and has many loves,*
And the broom's betrothed to the bee;
But I will plight with the dainty rose,
For fairest of all is she."

Thomas Hood

CHAPTER FIVE

Pests and Diseases

"*Those that plant should make their ground fit for rose trees before they set them, and not bury them in the ground like a dog. Let them have good and fresh lodgings suitable to their quality, and good attendance also, to preserve them from their enemies until they are able to encounter them.*"

Sir William Temple

Always start with strong, healthy, disease-resistant plants, then care for them well. Choose an appropriate site, prepare the soil, and plant the roses firmly. Once established, feed, mulch, water, and prune them regularly, and keep the beds free from debris. Never propagate from diseased plants, and always use organic or biological methods of prevention and cure.

BALLING
Symptoms: Buds develop but fail to open, turn brown.
Causes: Wet weather, aphid attacks, or excessive shade.
Some varieties more susceptible than others.

DIE BACK
Causes: Frost damage, mildew, or waterlogging.
Treatment: Avoid pruning and feeding in late summer
or autumn, which produce unripe, susceptible growth.

FROST DAMAGE
Symptoms: Leaves and shoots brown, withered. Not
serious in milder areas, prune affected growth in
spring.
Treatment: Give winter protection in coldest regions.

SPRAY DAMAGE
Symptoms: Stems twist, leaves twist and shrivel.
Cause: Drifting weed-killer spray.
Treatment: Remove affected growth.

BALLING

DIE BACK

FROST DAMAGE

SPRAY DAMAGE

*W*eeds may harbor pests and diseases, and will compete with the roses for light, moisture, and food. Remove them by hand, shallow hoeing, or by applying a contact weedkiller.

*R*oses, like all plants, may suffer from all manner of troubles. The most common problems are black spot, mildew, mineral deficiency, and attacks by aphids. Fortunately, however, these are usually unsightly rather than fatal. Diseases are caused by fungi, bacteria, viruses, or other microorganisms, and prevention is always better than cure. Apply the appropriate sprays early in the season, just as growth starts, and repeat every two weeks until the plants become dormant. Water in the morning, to allow time for the leaves to dry off during the day. A spring mulch prevents rain from splashing spores onto the roses and causing reinfection.

BLACK SPOT

Symptoms: Black fringed spots; yellowing leaves, which fall prematurely; in severe cases, roses become defoliated, weaken, and eventually die.

Treatment: Destroy affected leaves and debris; cut out diseased wood; dust or spray with sulfur from midsummer to leaf fall; improve air circulation; mulch in spring; apply sulfate of potash in late summer.

POWDERY MILDEW

Symptoms: Powdery white bloom on leaves, stalks, and buds; leaves wilt, curl, and fall prematurely.

Treatment: Remove and destroy affected growth and debris; improve air circulation; water and feed regularly; hose bushes weekly; spray with sulfur.

APHIDS

Symptoms: Shoots covered with black, red, brown, or green sap-sucking insects; leaves, buds, and flowers deformed.

Treatment: Spray with insecticidal soap or release lacewings and parasitic wasps.

Mineral Deficiencies

NITROGEN DEFICIENCY
Symptoms: Small, pale leaves with red spots.
Treatment: Apply a compound fertilizer.

IRON DEFICIENCY
Symptoms: Yellow patches on older leaves, young leaves all yellow.
Treatment: Apply sequestered iron.

PHOSPHATE DEFICIENCY
Symptoms: Small, dark leaves with purplish undersides.
Treatment: Apply a compound fertilizer.

POTASH DEFICIENCY
Symptoms: Reddish tint on young foliage; older leaves have dry, brittle edges.
Treatment: Apply a compound fertilizer.

MAGNESIUM DEFICIENCY
Symptoms: Pale-centered leaves with dead patches; leaves fall prematurely.
Treatment: Apply fertilizer containing magnesium.

MANGANESE DEFICIENCY
Symptoms: Yellow bands between leaf veins.
Treatment: Apply an appropriate fertilizer.

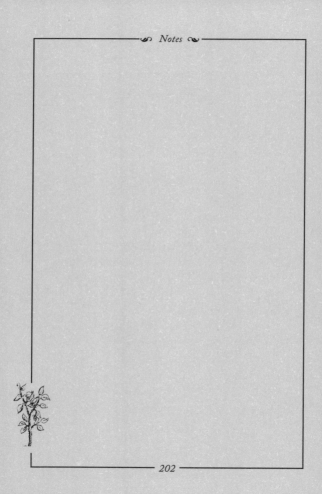

*M*any insects, including hoverflies, lacewings, ladybugs, parasitic wasps, and predatory mites, are beneficial in the garden. Some may be purchased, but attract all you can by growing their favorite plants and creating habitats for them, and by avoiding the use of sprays that will harm them. You can provide a winter home for lacewings with only a large plastic bottle and a piece of corrugated cardboard. Cut the bottom from the bottle and fill it with a roll of the cardboard, then hang it, open end down, in a tree. Some birds feed on aphids. Encourage them into the garden by hanging coconuts-halves, peanuts, or fat in trees and shrubs near the roses.

"Leave not the business of today to be done tomorrow ...
The rose garden which today is full of flowers,
tomorrow, when thou wouldst pluck a rose,
may not afford thee even one."

Firdawsi, from the ancient Persian.

CHAPTER SIX

The Rose Indoors

*"Then will I raise aloft the milk-white rose, with whose
sweet smell the air shall be perfumed."*

William Shakespeare

*F*or drying and preserving, cut perfect flowers, buds, and leaves early on a dry summer morning, when the dew has evaporated and before the sun climbs high. For potpourri, choose petals from just-opened roses. Gather hips when they are ripe and well-colored. Roses intended for culinary or medicinal use should be taken from unsprayed plants growing in unpolluted areas.

Drying

There are various methods for drying roses, depending on the purpose for which they are intended. Flowers for dried arrangements should be hung up to dry, while flower heads and petals should be dried flat. Perfect blooms for decoration are best dried in silica-gel crystals.

Hang-Drying

Remove all the thorns and most of the leaves. Arrange the roses in small bunches, with the heads staggered so that they don't touch one another, then tie each bunch together with a rubber band or a piece of string. Hang the bunches upside down in a dry, airy place, away from strong light.

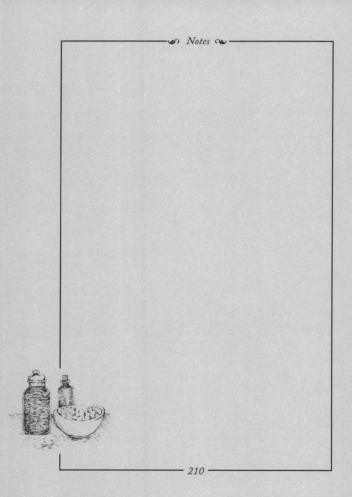

Drying Flat

Lay the flower heads and petals, spaced well apart, on absorbent paper in a warm, dry place, away from strong light, until they are crisp.

Silica Drying

Fill a container to one-third of its depth with silica-gel crystals. Position the flower heads face up, and press them gently into the crystals. Trickle in more crystals, until the flowers are completely covered. Cover the container with a lid and leave in a cool, dry place. Check the flowers every day, and as soon as they are dry, remove them with a slotted spoon. If they are left too long in the crystals they will become brittle.

Potpourri

All manner of things can be used to make potpourri, according to what you have available and the combination of ingredients that takes your fancy. You can mix flowers, leaves, and bark; fragrant herbs, such as bay leaves, rosemary, and thyme; spices, such cumin, cloves, and mace; and dried citrus rind. A few drops of an essential oil of your choice will enhance the fragrance and a fixative, such as dried orrisroot, will help to set and preserve it.

Preparing the Ingredients

To make a dry potpourri, strip leaves, tiny flower heads, and individual petals of larger flowers or herbs from their stems, and lay them out to dry. When dry, place each type in a separate storage jar and add a little powdered orrisroot to each. Continue to dry and add more, until you have enough. To dry citrus rind, scrape away any pith, thread the rind onto a length of cotton, and hang it up to dry in a warm place. For moist potpourri, which has a richer and longer-lasting fragrance, use fresh, or partly dried leaves, flowers, and herbs.

*Y*ou can use these ingredients to make either dry or moist potpourri:

4 cups of rose petals
1 cup of rose-geranium leaves
2 tablespoons of lavender flowers
2 or 3 pieces of cinnamon stick
1 scant teaspoon of crushed cloves
4 drops of rose oil
2 drops of jasmine oil
Dried peel of one orange, torn into small pieces
1 teaspoon of dried orrisroot
Small, dried rosebuds to decorate

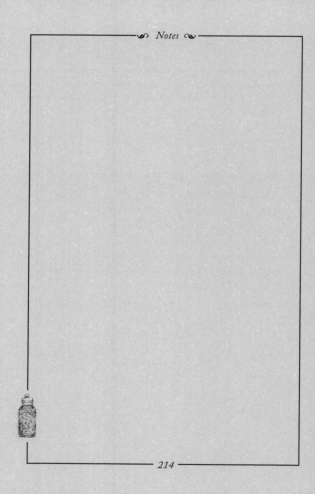

*F*or dry potpourri, tip all the dried flowers and leaves into a large mixing bowl. Throw in the pieces of cinnamon stick and sprinkle on the crushed cloves. Add the essential oils, the peel, and the orrisroot, and stir well. Store in a sealed container in a dark place for about six weeks, until the mixture has matured, shaking the container frequently. When the potpourri is ready, turn it out into bowls or specially made containers and decorate with the dried rosebuds.

*F*or moist potpourri, put a layer of petals, leaves, and lavender into a wide-mouthed jar, and frost with coarse sea salt. Continue to add ingredients as you harvest them until the jar is full, lightly sprinkling alternate layers with brown sugar and brandy. Weight down each addition. When the jar is full, seal it and leave the potpourri to mature for two months. Shake it frequently, and inspect the mixture occasionally—if it is too dry, add a little salt, if too wet, add some orrisroot. When a dryish cake has formed, turn it out into a bowl, crumble it gently, and add the spices, oils, rind, and fixative. Return the mixture to the jar, and leave it for another six weeks. When the potpourri is ready, turn it out into a container with a perforated lid.

Rose Oil

*F*ill a glass jar with scented rose petals, pressing them down until the jar is nearly full. Top up with light olive oil, cover, and leave to infuse for ten days, in the sun, if possible. Strain and add more petals to the oil. Repeat the process until you run out of petals, then strain, bottle, seal, and label.

Rose Syrup

*B*oil two cups of sugar, two cups of rose petals, and the juice and grated rind of one large lemon, in two cups of water, until the mixture is syrupy, then strain,

add rose water to taste, and a little red food coloring, if you like. Mix well, bottle, seal, and label. Use to flavor custards, fruit cups, ices, and sorbets

Sugared Rose Petals

Pick perfect petals from a fragrant rose just before it blooms, and snip off the white piece at the base of each petal. Brush the petals with lightly beaten egg white and place them on a sheet of waxed paper. Sprinkle one side with fine sugar, then turn them over and sprinkle the other side. Leave to dry in the sun, if possible, or in a heated closet (airing cupboard) or a very cool oven. When dry, store the petals in an airtight tin between layers of waxed paper.

Rose-Petal Jam

Fill a pan with petals from damask roses and cook slowly in a little water until the petals "melt." Weigh the pulp, and add an equal quantity of sugar and a little lemon juice, if you like. Heat slowly to dissolve the sugar, then bring to the boil, reduce the heat, and simmer gently until thick.

Rose-Scented Toilet Water

2 cups of distilled water
4 tablespoons of pure alcohol, or vodka
1 cup of scented rose petals
8 or more drops of rose oil

Steep the petals in the distilled water for two hours, then drain off the liquid and add the spirit. Pour into a bottle, add the rose oil, two or three drops at a time, shaking well after each addition.

Roses as House Plants

*U*ntil recently, roses were not considered suitable house plants because of their need for light and circulating air, although they were sometimes brought indoors for a few days of glory on special occasions. Nowadays, miniature roses are commonly grown as house plants and do well provided they are given a humid atmosphere and plenty of light. For best results, place a layer of gravel or small pebbles in a bowl and add water to come just below the level of the gravel. Stand the potted rose on the gravel and place it on a sunny windowsill, but where it can be shielded from hot midday sun. If possible, provide the rose with fluorescent lighting at night and on dark days. Keep it well watered, adding a liquid feed, but allow the pot to dry out between each watering. Mist spray regularly.

Roses as Cut Flowers

*F*or fresh indoor arrangements, pick roses in the evening and cut only those that are in bud, with the first petals just beginning to unfold. Take no more than one-third of each stem, from just above an outward-facing bud. Strip off the thorns, and any leaves that will be below the water in the vase, then cut the bottoms of the stems again, on a slant, with a sharp knife. Make a $1/2$ in (1.5cm) slit up each stem, or crush with a hammer. Stand the roses up to their necks in cold water, and leave overnight. In the morning, arrange them in a vase of fresh water. If the roses in a display begin to wilt, cut off the ends of their stems, then stand them in a few inches (centimeters) of boiling water for two minutes. Replace them in the vase, adding a teaspoon of sugar to the water.

A FRIEDMAN/FAIRFAX BOOK

© 1998 MQ Publications Ltd
© 1998 by Michael Friedman Publishing Group, Inc.

Library of Congress Cataloging-in-Publication Data available upon
request.

ISBN: 1-56799-613-2

Edited and produced by MQ Publications Ltd.
Text © Angela Kirby 1998
Illustrations © Anny Evason 1998
Editor: Linda Tsiricos
Designer: Bet Ayer

Printed in Hong Kong

1 3 5 7 9 10 8 6 4 2

For bulk purchases and special sales, please contact:
Friedman/Fairfax Publishers
Attention: Sales Department
15 West 26th Street
New York, New York 10010
212/685-6610   FAX 212/685-1307

Visit our website:
http://www.metrobooks.com